Dear Sadie, Soup for the Soul: A Journey through Breast Cancer

Sadie Jenkins

"The Lord gave the word: great was the company
of those that published it."
Psalms 68:11 (KJV)

Dedication

This book is dedicated to my family and close friends.

Thank You to the doctors; God blessed you with the knowledge and hands to perform the exams and surgeries. God has blessed you with medical knowledge and understanding of illnesses and diseases.

I want to share my journey through my illness and my healing. The world needs to know how prayer brought me through the tough times, and I want to encourage someone today that it can work for you, too.

I want to give you hope for those going through any sickness or disease, not just breast cancer. You can overcome anything, and you can be victorious with every storm you go through. God is still a healer when you trust and believe in Him. God is enormous compared to any cancer, disease, or illness we may encounter. God loves us unconditionally despite anything we are going through or may have happened in our lifetime.

Continue to trust Him, stay strong, don't give up, and don't faint; your miracle is closer than you think. Your healing is on the way. Receive it. Our heavenly Father is still the author of mercies and deliverance, and you will be set free, In Jesus' Name.

> "This, the first of miracles Jesus did in Cana of Galilee and manifested forth his glory."
> John 2:11 (Commentary)

Father, who raised Christ from the dead, Thank you for carrying my sickness and bearing all my pains. By your stripes, I'm healed. I will keep your words in my heart; they are my life. Thank you for being my healer and keeping my mind and heart at peace through this journey.

In the name of Jesus Christ,
the son of the living God.

Amen!

February 25, 2016

Dear Sadie's Soup for the Soul,

I left work feeling ill with a terrible headache. I tried to keep my eyes open just enough to see as I drove to the doctor's office.

Immediately, as I walked through my doctor's office doors, they realized something was seriously wrong. I was ill; the fact that I drove myself to the office in that state was beyond belief. Usually, I am very healthy; they were in disbelief but sprung into action to discover what was wrong with me. I was taken to the back right away. The doctor checked my blood pressure because it was the most logical thing to do since my head was hurting and my eyes were red. As suspected, my blood pressure was 190/150, which fell into the stroke range. This explained my headaches that were causing me excruciating pain.

Immediately, my doctor placed me on a medical leave of absence from work until she could figure

out how my pressure got so high, and she had the opportunity to normalize it.

Father God, Thank you for regulating my blood pressure and controlling my heartbeat. Thank you, Father, for surrounding me with your angels, who safely took me to my doctor's office. Thank you for loving me.

> ***My flesh and my heart faileth: But God is the strength of my heart, and my portion for ever.***
>
> ***Psalm 73: 26 (KJV)***

February 29, 2016

I had my follow-up today, and my blood pressure was still higher than usual. My doctor prescribed blood pressure medication to me. I will now be taking Amlodipine 20 mg daily.

> ***Yea, though I walk through the valley of the shadow of death, I will fear no evil: for thou art with me; Thy rod and thy staff they comfort me.***
>
> ***Psalm 23: 4 (KJV)***

Thank you, Father, for reminding me in my place of hopelessness; You are my comforter and healer. I began to declare that I would no longer be afraid, and at that moment, the fear started to escape me.

March 7, 2016

I had another follow-up appointment today to monitor my blood pressure. My doctor stated that it was getting better but still slightly higher than it should be. She wants to schedule a complete body examination. Now she's concerned about how this relatively healthy patient of hers, with average weight and height for her age, suddenly has this life-threatening issue.

Father, I trust that all is well with me. Even if I'm not physically well, I can take comfort in knowing all is well with my soul. I have faith that God has healed me completely of my sickness, whatever that may be.

Blessed is the man who trusts in the Lord, and whose hope is the Lord. For he shall be like a tree planted by the waters, which spreads out its roots by the river, and will not fear when heat comes; but its leaf will be green, and will not be anxious in the year of drought nor will cease from yielding fruit.

Jeremiah 17: 7-8 (NKJV)

March 15, 2016

Today, I'm having a different procedure, a more detailed examination with blood work. MRIs and Biopsies, a pock here and a prick there, who would have thought going to the doctor could be so exhausting? I had no idea. Just thinking about the different doctors and all the appointments makes me tired. Not being able to go anywhere right now gets me a little down.

> **My flesh and my heart may fail, but God is the strength of my heart and my portion forever.**
>
> **Psalms 73: 26 (NIV)**

Thank you, Father, for being my strength through my weakness. My body is exhausted, but my soul still fights to be strong. While trying to keep my mind at peace, I'm reminded where my help comes from.

March 16, 2016

Some of my appointments are only days apart. The drive to and from the doctor visits is tiresome, and I'm just about sick of all the biopsies, cutting, and needles.

> ***Cast your burden on the Lord, and He shall sustain you; He shall never permit the righteous to be moved.***
>
> ***Psalms 55: 22 (NKJV)***

This, too, shall pass. The God I serve is a burden bearer. It's God's responsibility to carry my worry, sadness, oppression, and anything that may be too difficult for me.

March 18, 2016

My general doctor found a lump in my right breast near my underarm. She thinks it may be cancer but wants to refer me to a breast specialist, a surgical oncologist, to be exact, to examine me further. She scheduled my appointment for March 21, 2016.

No matter the results, I will **STILL TRUST GOD**. I will not be moved; I will hold on to God's promises for my life.

For I know the thoughts that I think toward you, says the Lord, thoughts of peace and not of evil, to give you a future and a hope.

Jeremiah 29: 11 (NKJV)

March 21, 2016

I will have my biopsy today to get a tissue sample for testing to see if my lump is cancerous.

Today, I felt a little sad about what's happening in my body. I'm almost grateful that my blood pressure was high, or else I wouldn't have come to the doctor to begin with. If I hadn't suffered from those headaches, I wouldn't have stepped foot into the doctor's office and wouldn't have known about the lump in my breast. Through this revelation, I'm thankful to know that God is still in control.

The fear of the LORD is the beginning of wisdom: And the knowledge of the holy is understanding. For by me thy days shall be multiplied, And the years of thy life shall be increased.

Proverbs 9: 10-11 (KJV)

Confess your faults one to another, and pray one for another, that ye may be healed.

James 5: 16 (KJV)

But he was wounded for our transgressions, he was bruised for our iniquities: the chastisement of our peace was upon him; and with his stripes we are healed.

Isaiah 53: 5 (KJV)

And when he had called unto him his twelve disciples, he gave them power against unclean spirits, to cast them out, and to heal all manner of sickness and all manner of disease.

Matthew 10: 1 (KJV)

March 22, 2016

I had another appointment with my general doctor today.

To God be the Glory, my blood pressure is lower than the last couple of visits. However, I will have to continue with my meds.

What great news to know that I'm on a lower dosage now. My doctor originally placed me on 25mg of Amlodipine, but now, Glory to God, I'm only on 5mg.

A cheerful heart is good medicine, but a crushed spirit dries up the bones.

Proverbs 17: 22 (NIV)

March 24, 2016

I will remain optimistic as I go through this season of my life. I won't have a pity party nor allow anyone to have one for me. I will not surround myself with people who express sadness or speak negatively about my illness. I won't be moved; I believe God will and has already healed me.

I choose to be cheerful and in good spirits. I believe with my heart that my attitude will determine how quickly this will all be behind me.

By His stripes, we are healed.

Isaiah 53: 5 (NKJV)

March 28, 2016

It's been a week since my last appointment. Today, I have a visit with my primary doctor. Today, they will draw more blood and conduct a B-12, Vitamin D, Cholesterol, and stress test.

With all the appointments, I can't seem to travel or schedule time for family events. This saddens me, but I'm quickly reminded that God has me in the palm of His hands, and the battle is not mine but the Lord's.

---

*.... Can she feel no love
for the child she has borne?
But even if that were
possible, I would not forget
you!*

*See, I have written your
name on the palms of my
hands.....*

Isaiah 49: 15-16 (NLT)

March 29, 2016

Today's visit is with the Surgical Oncologist (Breast Specialist). I have been having MRIs, biopsies, and ultrasounds on my right breast for about a month to determine whether the lump is cancerous. Each procedure has come back with abnormalities. My doctor is unsure if it's cancerous, but she will call me again after further reviewing the sample.

She finally called me to schedule an appointment with the radiologist for one more biopsy and the final assessment of the cancer stage.

When evil darkens our world,
give us light. When despair numbs
our souls, give us hope. When we
stumble and fall, lift us up. When
doubt assails us, give us faith.
When ideals fade, give us vision.

When we lose our way, be our guide. That we may find serenity in your presence, and purpose in doing your will.

John D. Rayner

March 31, 2016

I have an appointment with the radiation doctor today for more imaging and another biopsy. Most of my time seems to be spent going to the doctor's office, which has become a daily part of my life since February. Welcome to my new normal, at least for a little while.

There is something different about today, but my mind is made up. I will not be moved by what I see or hear. Weeping may endure for a moment, but joy comes in the morning.

Prayer

Father God, you know my heart today and how I am struggling to endure one more moment of this adversity. It feels hard to believe You have good in store for me, but I trust You are working all things for my good and Your Glory. Strengthen me today.

Grow and mature me so that I lack nothing in my faith. Help me persevere. Bathe me in your love and peace when the suffering, waiting, and lack of control are hard to endure. Remind me often that You, Jesus, have already overcome the world, including this struggle of mine. I don't want to resist or reject your work any longer. Flood my heart today with trust and peace as I lean in and let You work in my life through this situation.

In the name of Jesus Christ, the son of the living God.

Amen!

1 p.m.

Many people have asked, several times, if not more, "Why did I get this terrible disease?" My response is the same as usual: I will not question God's plan.

This is a test, and God will get the Glory. I speak healing and deliverance over myself. **I AM ALREADY HEALED, IN JESUS NAME…** God has already said that this is not the end for me, and I believe Him. I have had visions of myself telling stories about my life to my grands and great-grands, and this is a story to be told: How I've overcome breast cancer?

I will continue to look unto Jesus, the Author and Finisher of my fate. I will trust God. This trial that has plagued my life is only a test so that others can see how merciful and gracious our God is: For us to see His remarkable and extraordinary healing power.

> *Trust in the LORD with all thine heart; And lean not unto thine own understanding. In all thy ways acknowledge him, And he shall direct thy paths.*
>
> *Proverbs 3: 5-6 (KJV)*

6 p.m.

I will walk in the peace that passes all understanding. Yea, though I walk through the valley of the shadow of death, I will fear no evil; for thou art with me; thy rod and thy staff, they shall comfort me. Therefore, I will meditate on the goodness of the Lord, day and night, for this is the day that the Lord has made; let us rejoice and be glad in it. For I fear not, for I am with you. "Be not dismayed," says the Lord, I am your God. I am not afraid of this ugly disease. I believe without a doubt that I'm already healed. Lord, You have healed the sick, cleansed the lepers, raised the dead, and cast out devils, so I know I can be healed. Freely ye have received, freely ye shall give.

In the Name of Jesus,
Amen!

April 1, 2016

It was approximately 4 p.m.; I got the phone call I'd been waiting for. I have stage 1 breast cancer. My cancer is sensitive to female hormones. My estrogen level didn't decrease as I got older, and extreme stress triggered the estrogen in my body. My God, this is how I developed cancer. I suspected I had cancer because of all the abnormalities that were showing up in my tests, but wow!

I sat down for a moment to soak it all in. I have breast cancer. Then, I quickly remembered that the God I serve has already healed me and that I will not be moved by what I see or hear.

I decree healing and good health over my body. By His stripes, I'm healed of any illness or disease that tries to take up residency in my body.

Heavenly Father, You are the ultimate Healer, the divine Surgeon, and the Miracle Worker who knows every intricate detail of my being. Today, I come before You with a grateful heart, acknowledging Your sovereignty over my life and the healing process I must undergo. Help me, Lord, embrace the uniqueness of my journey and not compare myself to others. Remind me that Your timing is perfect, explicitly tailored to my needs.

In Your loving care, I place my life and my healing process. Strengthen me, O God, and grant me the grace to be still, trusting in Your faithfulness. I pray this in the name of Jesus, our Savior and Redeemer.

Amen!

April 7, 2016

Today, I meet with the three doctors who will be caring for me through this entire process. They will discuss surgery options and explain exactly what stage one cancer means and what it will entail.

My doctors said, "Diagnose with invasive ductal carcinoma-breast cancer that invades the milk duct—clinical stage 1, sensitive to female hormones." This is all because of the high estrogen level in my body, which didn't slow down or decrease as I got older. For my age (51), most women had begun or were already going through menopause. I was nowhere near menopause, which explained why I was not experiencing hot flashes. The tumor is 2cm. (an inch) but did not spread to the lymph nodes. Thank God for that.

April 11, 2016

I thought I was done with the MRIs and biopsies.

My schedule for the next phase begins.
The Plan

- ❖ Bilateral Breast MRI- Monday at 11 a.m.
- ❖ Tentative Surgery- April 25, 2016, Right partial mastectomy and sentinel node biopsy. I will arrive at 7:30 a.m. to prep for surgery, beginning at 9 a.m.
- ❖ After surgery, I will meet with the chemotherapy doctor to discuss treatments. He will tell me which radiation or chemotreatment will work best for me or if I need both.
- ❖ After treatments, whichever I have, I will be placed on Tamoxifen, a hormonal therapy. Tamoxifen will eventually stop the flow of my menstrual cycle so I can begin menopause.

As I await my surgery date, every night before falling asleep, I place my hand on the lump and repeat these words:

I am the body of Christ; I am redeemed from the curse because Jesus bore my sicknesses and carried my diseases in his body. By His stripes, I am healed. I forbid any sickness or disease to operate in my body. Every organ and every tissue of my body functions in the perfection God created it to serve. I honor God with my body.

In the name of Jesus
Amen!

April 14, 2016

I had another visit with my primary care doctor today. She wants to monitor my blood pressure to make sure it is stable before my surgery.

With so many doctor visits and procedures, I can't make plans to travel with friends and family members. I'm having to miss out on activities with my grandkids. Sometimes, I feel my brain is more tired than my body, thinking about how much I'm away from my children and grandchildren.

April 17, 2016

No appointments today, which is good for a change. I know my doctors are doing what's best for my medical care; however, I'd rather not leave my house some days. Driving myself to and from doctor visits tends to weigh on me mentally and physically. But I don't allow myself to stay there long. Giving up is not an option. I am grateful; I'm doing as well as I am. I will continue to trust God through this process. To God be the Glory, forever and ever.

But unto you, that fear my name shall the Sun of righteousness arise with healing in his wings;

Malachi 4: 2 (KJV)

April 19, 2016

It's less than one week before my surgery.

I'm constantly going before the Lord, as always. Although I'm undergoing surgery, God has already healed me. I stand by my belief. After all, God gave the doctor the knowledge and medical intelligence. The Bible states that some illnesses and diseases are healed supernaturally, and some are healed with medicine. I thank God for His wisdom and understanding.

April 21, 2016

I am being prepped today for my surgery, which is four days away, by my oncologist. I'm getting a little anxious now that the surgery is near, but I'm not afraid.

I will trust in the Lord with all thine heart and all thine might. When life gives you so many reasons to cry, be afraid, or give up, show life you have more reasons to smile, press on, live, and most of all, Trust God. Lean not unto thine own understanding; In all thine ways acknowledge Him, and He shall direct thy paths.

April 22, 2016

O'God of heaven and earth, I commend to your compassionate regard that no healing is too complex or burdensome for you. If it be your will, I pray that You work miracles through the doctors You have appointed for my care. I pray You bless each doctor and their families.

In the Name of Jesus
Amen!

April 23, 2016

We are now two days away from my surgery.

Return, O'Lord, deliver my soul. Oh, save me for thy mercy's sake. Thank you, Father God, for never leaving me nor forsaking me. Thank you for always being a pleasant help in my time of need. Who forgiveth all thine iniquities, who healeth all diseases.

April 25, 2016

It's 6:30 a.m. Today is the Big Day!

I'm getting ready for surgery. I will arrive at Hilton Head MUSC Bluffton Medical Campus at 7:30 a.m. I'm going for a sentinel node biopsy for surgery scheduled for 9 a.m.

A sentinel node biopsy involves injecting radioactive tracer blue dye through the nipple and traveling through the body wherever the cancer cell may travel.

April 28, 2016

The surgery was successful. I'm glad this part is now far behind me. I will try to sit still during the healing process. It's been a few days since my surgery. I feel much better than I imagined I would feel this soon afterward.

God is so awesome. He keeps showing His power mightily.

May 10, 2016

I had my first follow-up visit today since my surgery with my breast specialist. Everything is well. My wounds have healed relatively quickly, my doctor said.

My next doctor's appointment will be with my radiation and chemotherapy doctor.

May 13, 2016

I met with my radiation oncologist today at the Lewis Cancer Center Pavilion in Savannah, GA. I had to get a mold made of my upper body because I must sit in the same position for every treatment, which is supposed to help.

I am a little disappointed today because I had to miss my mom's birthday dinner this evening.

May 16, 2016

This afternoon's visit is with my chemotherapy doctor. He will determine whether I get chemotreatments, radiation, or both. He would also determine how many weeks of treatment I would need. As he was beginning to discuss what chemo treatments would benefit me, he surprisingly had a disturbed look on his face as he stared at the computer screen. His look towards the screen was as if he had to make a double take and ensure he believed what he saw. I asked, "Why do you have that look on your face?" He replied, "I have a picture of the tumor found before surgery, and I'm now looking at the sample taken after surgery. The tumor before was about an inch, and it shrunk. Now it's the size of a tiny pea."

This was the first time I cried through this whole journey. To God be the Glory. I believed God would heal me, and He did. My doctor also said, "This is the healing power of God."

My doctor ruled out chemotreatments. There is a chart for the recommendation of chemotherapy treatment, which ranges from 1-100%. I fell into a shallow percentile rate, 11%, to be exact. Again, I chanted, Thank God! Thank God!

My doctor said, "Chemo will do you more harm than good." So go away! Chemo.

So, as of now, we will have eight weeks of radiation treatments beginning June 13, 2016. Following radiation, I will be placed on Tamoxifen daily for three to five years.

> This is the day that the Lord has made,
> I will rejoice and be glad in it.

May 20, 2016

Today, I met with my breast specialist. She wants to check my wounds and ensure my skin and wounds are healing properly before I begin radiation treatments. My skin and wounds have healed relatively quickly, she states.

June 9, 2016

Today, I will meet with chemo and radiation doctors for counseling on what to expect from radiation and what they need me to do before and after each treatment.

The doctors told me my skin would burn and darken from radiation. I will feel a little tired and weary afterward. Treatments are five days a week, Monday through Friday. During these weeks, no scented body wash, lotions, or deodorant. I can only use unscented Dove soap, corn starch instead of deodorant, and pure aloe vera gel to rub on my breast before and immediately after radiation to relieve some of the burning.

June 11, 2016

My treatments start in a couple of days.

Going through this journey, I had moments where I felt a little emotional because I was pretty much doing this alone. I chose to separate myself from those who tend to feel sorry or saddened by this trial I'm going through. From time to time, I still get asked, Why Me? I don't know, but I believe God chose me because He knew I wouldn't faint, get weary, or give up. He wants others to know He is still God in the midst, and good shall come out of this. God will get the Glory and show Himself to be mighty.

One thing I'm sure of, I'm glad that I had a relationship with God before being diagnosed with breast cancer. It's an incredible thing to be able to hear God's voice and to speak back to Him. My faith has made this journey easier to bear. Of course, I had moments, but then I realized God was going through this with me.

Therefore, since we have been justified through faith, we have peace with God through our Lord Jesus Christ, through whom we have gained access by faith into this grace in which we now stand. And we boast in the hope of the glory of God. Not only so, but we also glory in our sufferings, because we know that suffering produces perseverance; perseverance, character; and character, hope.

Romans 5: 1-4 (NIV)

June 13, 2016

I had my first radiation treatment this evening. I felt a little weak afterward, but I'm good.

Even though I walk through the darkest valley, I will fear no evil, for you are with me; your rod and your staff, they comfort me.

Psalms 23: 4 (KJV)

June 17, 2016

It's been a week of treatments so far. Life is different for me now. I look at my life and others with even more compassion than I had before.

I choose not to worry about things I cannot change, focus on what I can, and I will continue to pray. God, keep my mind on You. God gives me the strength to continue to leap over these hurdles and any challenging time that lies ahead. I will focus on God's plans for my life: to be in good health, prosper, and not be harmed.

June 24, 2016

I got through another week of treatments. My breasts are starting to burn, and they are getting sore from the radiation, as expected. I'm buying a lot of aloe vera gel these days. It seems to help with the burning sensation.

Nonetheless, I am grateful for doing as well as I am. I shall not be moved. God has given me a sense of peace about this right from the beginning. His praises will continually be in my mouth.

In Ephesians 6, God instructs us to take the sword of the Spirit, which is the word of God, and pray in the Spirit at all times, on every occasion, in every season. In these moments, we shall overcome.

July 1, 2016

Hello, good people,

Woo-Hoo! I have completed another week of radiation treatments. My skin has burnt a little more, but I feel great. My doctors are still in awe at how well I'm healing, which is quicker than they anticipated. As always, my response is, Thank you, God, for all You're doing, and To You, God be the Glory.

July 8, 2016

I woke up this morning reflecting on how good God is. He has never left me nor forsaken me. He's still in the miracle-working business. He's still a healer and deliverer.

Thank God for another week of radiation that is now behind me.

July 13, 2016

The Radiation Oncologist told me, **"Today Will Be My Last Treatment.** My body has healed relatively quickly, and there is no need to go through any more radiation."

Thank God I got done three weeks earlier than the doctors originally scheduled me. The staff held a little graduation ceremony for me and handed me a certificate of completion of Radiation Therapy.

This is the day the Lord has made. I will rejoice, and I am glad in it! I rejoice in You always, and again I say, I rejoice. I delight myself in You, Lord; happy am I because God is my Lord.

Amen!

July 18, 2016

I'm going to see my chemo doctor; they want to check my skin to see if there are any tears in my skin. He's also prescribing the Tamoxifen pill, decreasing my estrogen level and making me start menopause.

August 19, 2016

I've been taking the Tamoxifen pills for a couple of weeks now. I woke up drenched in sweat. I didn't know I could even sweat that much. If waking up in night sweats is good for me, I will have to learn to cope with it. I don't remember sweating this much when I ran ten to fifteen miles daily. It's all good as long as the hot flashes are helping my body. All that I have gone through was necessary. I am humbly grateful!

In my mind, heart, and most of all, in my spirit, I believed God would heal me of cancer. With great faith and God, I knew the outcome would be victorious. I trusted that if I gave this battle to God, He would move mightily, and He did. Even when people looked at me like I was an alien from out of space, I trusted God. Through it all, I kept saying God would heal me, and He did. I have no regrets about traveling on this road. I'm grateful for all the doctor's visits, which were sometimes two in one day or days apart. This battle was not mine, but the journey was.

All that I am and all I have is because of the Lord, who has favored my life.

Praise be to God in the highest!
Amen!

Dear Sadie's Soup for the Soul,

Sometimes, life throws us a curve ball. Depending on the situation, it tends to make us think differently. We tend to lose faith and hope and may even become afraid. But when I think about the pain and suffering Jesus Christ endured on the cross. My Prayer Life, Hope, and Faith strengthen again. The renewing of our minds Powers us to maintain our faith and anchors our thinking and God's words. The renewing of our minds helps us build our trust, which unveils the perspective of God, His miracles, and possibilities for our lives.

However, there will always be challenges and obstacles in our lives. But our faith and belief in God to heal our bodies from sicknesses, diseases, or any other obstacles we may face are all we truly need to conquer.

Ephesians 4:23
Be renewed in the spirit and your mind.

About the Author

Sadie Jenkins is a mother and grandmother who lives in Ridgeland, SC. She has over 30 years of experience in the Food and Beverage Industry, the last 20 of which have been as a Chef or Executive Chef. While participating in the Ultimate Chef of America Competition, she and her team won Best Presentation and Overall Taste.

Sadie is also the proud owner of Painting with Sadie.

Sadie Jenkins is an author and a fearless woman of God.

Praise the Lord, my soul;
All my inmost being, praise his holy name.
Praise the Lord, my soul,
And forget not all his benefits-
Who forgives all your sins
And heals all your diseases,
Who redeems your life from the pit
And crowns you with love and compassion.

Psalms 103:1-4 (NIV)

9 7 9 8 2 1 8 4 7 3 2 7 3